SAN FRANCISCO
THE CITY AT A GLANCE

C000084914

Transamerica Pyramid
At 260m tall, the city's most re
skyscraper towers over the Fin
It is no longer home to the Tra
corporation, but the name has
See p013

City Hall
A Beaux Arts gem topped by a gilded dome,
this core building of the Civic Center had
to be restored after the 1989 earthquake.
It reopened in 1999 in all its former glory.
1 Dr Carlton B Goodlett Place

Ferry Building
Until the 1930s, this was where most people
arrived in town. These days, it's the location
of a sprawling marketplace trading in local
meat, cheese and assorted produce.
The Embarcadero/Market Street

Market Street
Running diagonally north-east from The
Castro up to the Ferry Building, Market
Street is a main route for San Francisco's
famous fleet of renovated cable cars.

SFMOMA
Mario Botta's highly distinctive design for the
city's destination art venue is being added
to by Snøhetta. A bigger, more integrated
museum complex will be unveiled in 2016.
151 3rd Street, T 357 4000

Bay Bridge
This 7,180m-long crossing is actually two
spans in one, connected by Yerba Buena
Island. Its cantilevered eastern half was
damaged in the latest major earthquake,
and rebuilt at an estimated cost of $6.4bn,
before opening again in September 2013.

INTRODUCTION
THE CHANGING FACE OF THE URBAN SCENE

One of the most cosmopolitan and alluring cities in America, San Francisco is endowed with a liberal mindset and a knockout setting. Its numerous anomalies – Victorian architecture and radical new builds cheek by jowl; 19th-century cable cars running alongside cutting-edge hybrid vehicles; the technorati colliding with dyed-in-the-wool social activists – all make for an enthralling mix. Less daunting and less aggressive than New York, and more compact than Los Angeles, San Francisco is comparatively easy to navigate. Its diverse tribes stick to well-defined neighbourhoods, from the monied Nob Hill and Pacific Heights, to the emerging Dogpatch.

This tech boomtown is forever looking towards the next IPO, despite a growing concern about the effects of these new fortunes. Spirited debates circle around skyrocketing house prices, and the consequent displacement of artists and the working class. In Mid-Market – which, thanks to the Twitter tax break of 2011, is now *the* place to live, work, and play for those that can afford it – glossy condo complexes are springing up alongside shuttered storefronts.

San Francisco's dynamic cultural life is cause for optimism, from the grassroots scene to major projects such as the transformation of SFMOMA (see p032). Infrastructure and public spaces are also being upgraded. The Transbay Transit District (see p064) and the mixed-use development 950-974 Market, designed by the Bjarke Ingels Group, are hopeful indicators of a city with a bright future.

ESSENTIAL INFO
FACTS, FIGURES AND USEFUL ADDRESSES

TOURIST OFFICE
900 Market Street
T 391 2000
www.sanfrancisco.travel

TRANSPORT
Airport transfer to city centre
Trains depart regularly from 4am until midnight on weekdays, and from 6am on Saturdays and 8am on Sundays. The journey takes approximately 30 minutes
www.bart.gov
Cable cars and trolleybuses
Muni
www.sfmta.com
Car hire
Avis
T 929 2555
Taxi
Yellow Cab Cooperative
T 333 3333
Tourist card
A seven-day CityPASS ($86) includes travel on Muni transport and free entry to select attractions such as Alcatraz (see p035)
www.citypass.com/san-francisco

EMERGENCY SERVICES
Emergencies
T 911
24-hour pharmacy
Walgreens
459 Powell Street
T 984 0793
www.walgreens.com

CONSULATES
British Consulate
Suite 850
1 Sansome Street
T 617 1300
www.gov.uk/government/world/usa

POSTAL SERVICES
Post office
150 Sutter Street
T 765 1761
Shipping
UPS
T 775 6644

BOOKS
A Crack in the Edge of the World: The Great American Earthquake of 1906
by Simon Winchester (Penguin)
Tales of the City
by Armistead Maupin (Black Swan)
This is San Francisco
by Miroslav Sasek (Universe)

WEBSITES
Art/Design
www.fecalface.com
www.sfarts.org
Newspaper
www.sfgate.com

EVENTS
San Francisco Design Week
www.sfdesignweek.org
San Francisco International Film Festival
www.sffs.org/festival-home

COST OF LIVING
Taxi from SFO Airport to city centre
$60
Cappuccino
$4
Packet of cigarettes
$7
Daily newspaper
$1
Bottle of champagne
$75

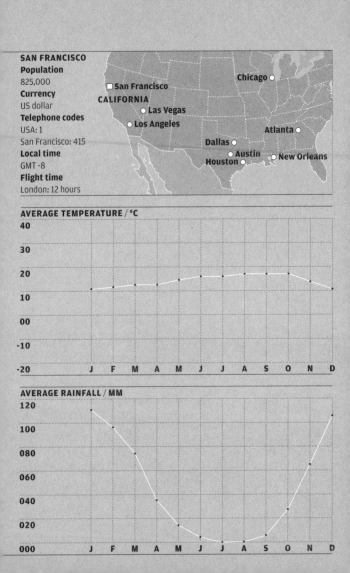

SAN FRANCISCO
Population
825,000
Currency
US dollar
Telephone codes
USA: 1
San Francisco: 415
Local time
GMT -8
Flight time
London: 12 hours

San Francisco
CALIFORNIA
Las Vegas
Los Angeles
Chicago
Atlanta
Dallas
Austin
Houston
New Orleans

AVERAGE TEMPERATURE / °C

40												
30												
20												
10												
00												
-10												
-20	J	F	M	A	M	J	J	A	S	O	N	D

AVERAGE RAINFALL / MM

120												
100												
080												
060												
040												
020												
000	J	F	M	A	M	J	J	A	S	O	N	D

NEIGHBOURHOODS

THE AREAS YOU NEED TO KNOW AND WHY

To help you navigate the city, we've chosen the most interesting districts (see below and the map inside the back cover) and colour-coded our featured venues, according to their location; those venues that are outside these areas are not coloured.

NORTH BEACH

In the city's north-eastern corner, where the hilltop art deco Coit Tower (see p010) keeps a beady eye on proceedings, North Beach and Telegraph Hill are packed with restaurants and bars. San Francisco's main theatre and comedy venues are also here.

NOB HILL

This is where the gold and silver barons flocked in the 1800s, in order to be above the hoi polloi. The neighbourhood looks over the Financial District, Russian Hill and the Bay. The Fairmont (see p016) and Grace Cathedral (1100 California Street, T 749 6300) are notable residents.

HAIGHT-ASHBURY

Surely the most famous cross street in the US, Haight-Ashbury is now a sad pastiche, full of relics from its psychedelic heyday and teens searching for the ghosts of the beatniks and Grateful Dead. A few venues have attempted to steer the area in a new direction, but it's best viewed for what it once stood for, not what it has become.

SOMA

South of Market Street, or SoMa, is the city's cultural epicentre, encompassing SFMOMA (see p032), Yerba Buena Center for the Arts (see p032) and the Museum of the African Diaspora (685 Mission Street, T 358 7200), as well as stylish hotels like the Zetta (see p017) and the W (see p018). Mid-Market is the new quarter to watch.

CHINATOWN

A bustling downtown hub, this is the largest Chinatown outside Asia. Enter via its famed gate and explore its streets and alleyways, which are crowded but captivating. The Sichuan cuisine at Z&Y (655 Jackson Street) is top-notch.

THE CASTRO

As the heart of the West Coast's gay scene, The Castro seems too outré to be true. But this is the most liberal neighbourhood in America's most liberal city, so leave your prejudices at the door and enjoy the show. Unsurprisingly, you'll find some of the best clubs and bars here, so do explore.

THE MISSION

San Francisco's hottest artists, hippest hostelries and eateries, and edgier shops are situated in this creative district; check out restaurants such as Mission Chinese Food (2234 Mission Street, T 863 2800). The area is named after Mission Dolores, the oldest building in town, and the Latino community here remains strong.

HAYES VALLEY

Located between the Civic Center to the east and Alamo Square to the west, this fashionable zone spreads out from Hayes Street. Among the quarter's multitude of interesting shops we like the fashion retailer MAC (387 Grove Street, T 863 3011) and the florist-cum-magazine store Birch (564 Hayes Street, T 626 6860).

LANDMARKS
THE SHAPE OF THE CITY SKYLINE

San Francisco is something of a landmark itself, for everything it suggests and personifies about the American psyche. Imbued with cool and charm, it's also a sight to behold, especially when viewed from either the Bay or the monumental Golden Gate Bridge (see p012), with the Californian sun illuminating its buildings. Driving up and down the city's rollercoaster streets, it's easy to understand why Steve McQueen's Frank Bullitt, careering around in his green Mustang, is hailed as the hippest cop ever to appear on screen.

Hemmed in on three sides by water, San Francisco has always grown vertically, the only way it could. As a result, the splendour of the 19th-century architecture that survived the calamitous 1906 earthquake (most of the city was already destroyed by the time the resulting fire was put out) has been swallowed up downtown by bland, formulaic skyscrapers. One that stands out from the crowd, however, is the gleaming, quartz-fronted Transamerica Pyramid (see p013) by William L Pereira; it can be seen from most parts of town, acting as a useful orientation point.

San Francisco has its fair share of unusual landmarks too. For instance, Lombard Street (see p034) draws coachloads of tourists ready to be amazed by its sine-wave windings. And although the Dutch Windmill at Ocean Beach (1691 John F Kennedy Drive) is not as well known internationally, it's still beloved by locals.
For full addresses, see Resources.

Coit Tower
The 64m art deco Coit Tower stands on top of Telegraph Hill's Pioneer Park, and affords visitors some of the finest views of the Bay from its rotunda. Built using funds left to the city by a wealthy financier's widow, Lillie Hitchcock Coit, it was finished in 1933. Inside, local artists have created murals that depict the Great Depression. *1 Telegraph Hill Boulevard, T 831 2791*

Golden Gate Bridge

One of the planet's great architectural icons, the Golden Gate Bridge is instantly recognisable and, when seen first-hand, its power remains undiminished. The 2.7km structure spans the Pacific Ocean where it meets San Francisco Bay, its two huge towers rising 227m above the water, joining the city to Marin County. Finished in 1937, four years after the first foundations were anchored, it was originally going to be painted black and yellow, but leading architect Irving F Morrow insisted on the now-irreplaceable international orange. The bridge seems to accentuate its own myth, as it is often shrouded in fog rolling in off the ocean, or bathed in dappled Californian sunshine. Driving across it in a convertible is surely one of the best experiences in the world.

T 921 5858, www.goldengatebridge.org

Transamerica Pyramid

William L Pereira's 48-floor skyscraper, which was completed in 1972, dominates the Financial District and beyond, serving as a handy navigational aid. Nicknamed Pereira's Prick by its detractors, it faced fierce opposition during its planning and construction, but the building is now as synonymous with San Francisco as the Golden Gate Bridge. The Transamerica Pyramid is covered in crushed quartz, which gives it a white appearance, and when seen from across the Bay on a sunny day, it does appear to glow. Following the 9/11 attacks, an observation deck towards the 260m summit was closed, but large video screens in the plaza-level visitors' centre display live views from cameras mounted at the top of the spire.

600 Montgomery Street,
www.thepyramidcenter.com

Federal Building
This slender government edifice was designed by Morphosis, architects of the Caltrans District 7 headquarters in downtown Los Angeles. The most radical architecture to appear in the heart of the city for decades, the 2007 Federal Building divided local opinion, but a year after it opened won a Design Award from San Francisco's AIA chapter. *Mission Street/7th Street*

HOTELS

WHERE TO STAY AND WHICH ROOMS TO BOOK

Study its skyline cluttered with cranes, and you'll see the city is in the midst of a boom. In spite of San Francisco's liberal leanings, the local hotel market has traditionally been staid, but is now at the forefront of much of this new development. Underway is a highly anticipated revamp of Mid-Market's Renoir Hotel, a multimillion-dollar project that will include a cool rooftop bar. Meanwhile, the scene remains conservative. There have been other renovations, of the Mandarin Oriental (222 Sansome Street, T 276 9888) and The Fairmont (950 Mason Street, T 772 5000), for example, but nothing that approaches the adventurous concepts you'll find in, say, London or New York. That said, there are novel experiences to be had, such as the anime-inspired Hotel Tomo (1800 Sutter Street, T 921 4000) and former army-officer quarters of the Inn at the Presidio (42 Moraga Avenue, T 800 7356).

Many of the better hotels are in the east of town: the splendid old mansion blocks of Nob Hill, the business options along Market Street and The Embarcadero, and the modern offerings of SoMa. As Mid-Market continues to gentrify, it's surely only a matter of time before this area sees the launch of more exciting boutique hotels, such as Union Square's Hotel G (see p021). If you're keen to be green, opt for the luxe but LEED-certified Orchard Garden (466 Bush Street, T 399 9807), the city's first eco-friendly hotel. *For full addresses and room rates, see Resources.*

Hotel Zetta

Making the most of the tech boom, the Viceroy Group opened its first property in San Francisco in 2013, taking over the former Hotel Milano. Following a $13m revamp, it's now a brogrammers' paradise, kitted out with a mezzanine gaming room, Jambox speakers and bluetooth TVs, as well as retro-nostalgic decor – look out for the pop-art portraits made from floppy discs. The 116 guest rooms (Premier Studio King, above) were transformed into urban lofts by the Seattle-based Dawson Design Associates. Book a suite and you'll have access to a wet bar, Nintendo Wii U games, and vinyl to play on Crosley turntables. Downstairs, the S&R Lounge is a cool spot to hold meetings, and the gastropub-style Cavalier has a hidden members-only bar.
55 5th Street, T 543 8555,
www.hotelzetta.com

W

Adjacent to the San Francisco Museum of Modern Art (which is undergoing a major expansion until 2016), this is one of the more design-forward hotels in the city. The rooms are accented with bright blues, vibrant oranges and patterned upholstery, and feature contemporary furnishings. Among the most flamboyant is the 65 sq m Fantastic Suite (opposite), which has a living room and two bathrooms. A calmer interior would be one of the Cool Corner Rooms, which are done out with darkwood panelling, Chinese-inspired art, and, in some cases, views over Yerba Buena Gardens. Come cocktail hour, head to the Stanley Saitowitz-designed Living Room Bar, which has an inviting fireplace and lounge area (above). If the hotel's party atmosphere gets too much, retreat to its indoor pool or Bliss Spa (T 817 4101).
181 3rd Street, T 777 5300,
www.wsanfrancisco.com

Hotel G

The location is central, yet hotels have
previously launched here without much
success. Hotel G, opened in 2014, seems
to have the formula right. The renovation
of the art deco building by New York firm
Hun Aw Studio has been deftly handled,
to reveal the original cross bracing and
a glorious cast-iron staircase. There's
an authentic San Francisco feel too; the
artwork is curated by Creativity Explored,
a non-profit gallery and studio for artists
with developmental disabilities. Stylishly
done, the interiors include refurbished
Victorian sofas and vintage wallpaper.
The 153 rooms, such as the Greatest King
(left), have a cool but sophisticated North
Californian aesthetic, with walnut finishes,
muted colours and hand-dyed rugs. Waxed
canvas pouches, by Strawfoot Handmade,
make a nice alternative to a minibar.
386 Geary Street, T 738 0589,
www.hotelgsanfrancisco.com

Hotel Vertigo

After a $5m transformation, the York Hotel re-emerged as the Vertigo in 2009, taking its new name from the Hitchcock film that made the location famous (Kim Novak's character, Judy Barton, lived in the building, then the Empire Hotel). It's a charming option, with a whimsical edge. The decor combines an orange, white and aubergine palette with oversized furniture, antiques, pop sculptures and horse-head lamps, as seen in the Executive King room (above). Designer Thomas Schoos should be applauded for embracing the Hitchcock theme and running with it in a tasteful way. Art inspired by the movie is dotted around, and of course a large flatscreen TV in the lobby shows 'Vertigo' on a loop – handy for any plot twists you may have missed. *940 Sutter Street, T 885 6800, www.hotelvertigosf.com*

Mystic Hotel

Although it launched in 2009 (as The Crescent), and was refurbished in 2012, the Mystic Hotel feels as if it's been here in this Victorian building for decades. Rooms, such as the Mystic Junior Suite (above), feature minibars stocked with wine from small Californian labels, and there's a nicely curated selection of books nestled amid the original wainscoting and bay windows. A popular spot with locals, the tucked-away Burritt Room bar, which has exposed brick walls and comfy leather sofas, is another highlight. Named after the Nob Hill alley where Miles Archer was murdered in the 1941 film *The Maltese Falcon*, it serves great cocktails, which you can savour without the scrum of other hostelries in the area. *417 Stockton Street, T 400 0500, www.mystichotel.com*

Clift

The 19th-century exterior of the Clift belies the fact that, inside, hotelier Ian Schrager and designer Philippe Starck have gone to town in trademark fashion. Oversized furniture and striking throws pepper the lobby, which opens on to the Velvet Room restaurant (T 929 2300), and the stunning Redwood Room (T 929 2372), one of the city's most impressive watering holes. The accommodations are pared-down Starck, decorated in shades of lavender and grey, but comfortable and elegant nonetheless, with carefully considered details including state-of-the-art sound systems and luxuriant bedding. Standard options, like 309 (above), are pleasant, but the Studio Rooms are more spacious and represent better value.
495 Geary Street, T 775 4700,
www.clifthotel.com

St Regis

Opened in 2005, San Francisco's St Regis is one of the brand's chicest properties. Situated at the heart of vibrant SoMa, it has an award-winning restaurant, Ame (T 284 4040), the first-class Remède Spa (T 284 4060), and a butler service. Grain-matched dark Mozambique hardwood lines the hallways, and the 2.4m doors open on to light-filled rooms with pale stitched-leather walls, crisp linens, and bedside control panels. The St Regis also displays some of its own art collection, including works by international and local artists, such as Stephen De Staebler's *Winged Woman on One Leg III* sculpture. From the eighth-floor Superior Rooms (above), you'll have a fantastic panorama of the surrounding cityscape.

125 3rd Street, T 284 4000,
www.stregissanfrancisco.com

Hotel Vitale

A 200-room luxury venture located at the eastern end of Mission Street, directly opposite the Ferry Building on the waterfront, the Vitale opened in 2005. Accommodation ranges from Deluxe City View Rooms to the Cielo Terrace Suite, which has a large private terrace (pictured) overlooking the Bay. Most of the guest rooms are bright and flooded with sunlight, and the decor is minimal and chic. The hotel is geared towards helping guests relax: there are free daily yoga classes, two rooftop hot tubs to banish any residual stress, and Spa Vitale (T 278 3788) on the penthouse level. There's also an excellent bar/restaurant, Americano (T 278 3777), which gets packed on week nights.
8 Mission Street, T 278 3700,
www.hotelvitale.com

Taj Campton Place

This venerable boutique hotel became one of only three Taj Hotels in the US in 2007, and the group has been gradually upgrading the property ever since. There are 110 rooms and suites, some boasting super views of nearby Union Square. The decor is uninspiring if inoffensive: colours are earthy but soothing, and furnishings veer towards the traditional. If you have the budget, the top-floor Luxury Suite 1702 (above) has a library and dining room. The in-house restaurant, which serves Californian cuisine with a Mediterranean spin, was awarded a Michelin star in 2011. Helmed by chef Srijith Gopinathan, it's an elegant setting, but those in the know head to the hotel's bistro/bar, one of the city's secrets, revered for its burgers. *340 Stockton Street, T 781 5555, www.tajhotels.com*

Palace Hotel

One of the oldest and most beautiful hotels in the city, the Palace, like The Fairmont (see p016) weathered the great earthquake of 1906 and, thanks to some serious renovation, now looks as splendid as it did when it opened in 1875. Even if you're not a guest here, the spectacular 80,000-pane stained-glass atrium in the Garden Court, replete with chandeliers and marble columns, is a must-see. There are 553 rooms, including 34 suites, such as the Chancellor (above), and although they don't match the grandeur of the atrium, they do boast four-poster beds, plush furnishings and tasteful artwork. The Pied Piper Bar & Grill (T 546 5089) is adorned with a Maxfield Parrish mural, entitled *The Pied Piper of Hamelin*. *2 New Montgomery Street, T 512 1111, www.sfpalace.com*

InterContinental

Towering over the SoMa district is the InterContinental, one of the greenest hotels in California, with solar panels to boost power generation and an aluminium exterior that aids temperature control. Floor-to-ceiling windows on each floor maximise natural light and also provide stunning views throughout the hotel, enlivening the experience in the otherwise plainly decorated rooms. Of the 550 to choose from, we like the One-Bedroom Corner Suite 3006 (above). The sleek lobby (opposite) encompasses Bar 888, which specialises in grappa, and gets packed with the after-work crowd. The restaurant is unimpressive, but The Spa (T 616 6597), staffed by some of the best masseuses in town, is not to be missed. *888 Howard Street, T 616 6500, www.intercontinentalsanfrancisco.com*

24 HOURS
SEE THE BEST OF THE CITY IN JUST ONE DAY

San Francisco has much to offer the visitor, and its compact size makes it easy to explore; you can cross the city by car in half an hour. Public transport is efficient, and cable cars and trams provide a fun and historic way to get around town. If the weather's fine, take in the views from the water as well as land. Start at Sightglass (opposite), before negotiating the hairpins of Lombard Street (see p034) en route to Fisherman's Wharf, where ferries to Alcatraz (see p035) depart. Back on shore, have lunch at Bouli Bar (see p050).

SFMOMA (151 3rd Street, T 357 4000) is shut until 2016 – its collection has been dispersed among other institutions including Yerba Buena Center for the Arts (701 Mission Street, T 978 2700) and Oakland's Museum of California (1000 Oak Street, T 510 318 8400). In former warehouse district Potrero Hill, and neighbouring Dogpatch, the indie scene is thriving, notably in the galleries on Utah Street (see p037) and Potrero Avenue. Dogpatch's retail artery, 3rd Street, is accessible via the Light Rail: get off near the Museum of Craft and Design (No 2569, T 773 0303), stopping for a drink at Yield Wine Bar (No 2490, T 401 8984), or some ice cream at Mr and Mrs Miscellaneous (699 22nd Street, T 970 0750). One of the most sought-after, albeit pricey, dinner reservations is Saison (see p038). Console yourself afterwards with a late-night cocktail at Trick Dog (3010 20th Street, T 471 2999) or The Abbott's Cellar (see p041). *For full addresses, see Resources.*

09.00 Sightglass

Brothers Jerad and Justin Morrison established Sightglass in 2009, working out of a modest espresso kiosk. The pair slowly transformed the surrounding building into a café and coffee roaster, unveiling the results in 2011. Three years on, they opened a second outlet on 20th Street in The Mission (T 641 1043). The industrial wood-and-steel interior of the original venue was conceived by local designers Boor Bridges, and centres on a huge iron Probat roaster. Incredibly, given this is California, there's no wi-fi, which encourages customers to savour one of the best cups of coffee in the city. Order with a pistachio and blackberry croissant, supplied by baker Greg Mindel of Neighbor, and you won't miss it. *270 7th Street, T 861 1313, www.sightglasscoffee.com*

10.00 Lombard Street

After breakfast, head over to this local landmark (which is one-way), and wind along the 'crookedest street in the United States'. The famous snake-like section was created in 1922 at the suggestion of San Francisco real-estate owner and businessman Carl Henry, to tackle the steep hill's natural 27-degree slope, which presented big problems for vehicles and pedestrians used to more manageable inclines. If you don't drive down, the best view is from Leavenworth Street, looking up (above). While you're in the area, call into City Lights bookstore (T 415 362 8193), which is housed in a 1907 building and was a haunt of the Beats. Continuing the literary theme, Dorka Keehn and Brian Goggin's 'flock of books' sculpture, *The Language of the Birds*, is nearby on the corner of Columbus and Broadway.

10.30 Alcatraz

Make your way over to Fisherman's Wharf as early as possible, before it gets clogged with tourists, and board the Hornblower Hybrid ferry to Alcatraz (reserve a ticket in advance, especially in peak season). Tours of the world-famous penitentiary complex, which was in operation from 1934 to 1963, offer moving audio accounts of prisoners' lives there, and once on The Rock, as it's known, you'll understand how impossible it was to escape: jagged cliffs and shark-infested waters awaited anyone who was cunning enough to slip out of their cell. The views looking back towards the city merit the trip alone. Until April 2015, another draw is @Large, a series of site-specific installations located across the island by Chinese artist Ai Weiwei. *Alcatraz Cruises, Pier 33, Alcatraz Landing, T 981 7625, www.alcatrazcruises.com*

13.00 Pier 24

Andy and Mary Pilara sparked their passion for photography with their first purchase, an image by Diane Arbus from Fraenkel Gallery (T 981 2661) in 2003. Seven years later, they launched Pier 24, which holds 4,000 photographs, making it one of the world's largest collections of the medium. The 2,600 sq m warehouse space is climate-controlled, and visitors are limited to 20 at a time; entry is free, but appointments must be booked online. Exhibitions are themed and draw on the Pilaras' trove of canonical photographers (Walker Evans, Richard Avedon, William Eggleston), contemporary practitioners (Wolfgang Tillmans, Katy Grannan, Todd Hido) and emerging talent like Eric William Carrol (*Blue Line of Woods* diazotypes, above). Open Monday to Thursday. *Embarcadero, T 512 7424, www.pier24.org*

15.00 Catharine Clark Gallery

Bringing a big-city edge to the SF scene, Catharine Clark is a leader in exhibiting experimental video art, and the first gallery in town to feature a multimedia room. Showcasing contemporary work in six-week-long exhibits, the space displays a roster of established artists working in the local area and beyond. These have included sculptor Andy Diaz Hope, and Deborah Oropallo, known for paint-and-digital depictions of livestock, as seen in her collaboration with Michael Goldin, *Milk Made* (above). In late 2013, the gallery relocated to a former factory in Potrero Flats, bolstering a burgeoning art community there: Hosfelt Gallery (T 495 5454); Wattis Institute (T 355 9670); Yves Béhar's Fused Space (1401 16th Street). *248 Utah Street, T 399 1439, www.cclarkgallery.com*

19.00 Saison

Serving ultra-local New American cuisine, Saison won its first Michelin star in 2011 and a second the following year. In 2013, the restaurant moved into the California Electric Light Company Building, which was completed in 1888 and survived the 1906 earthquake. Architects Michael Gibson and Samaha+Hart, in collaboration with interior designer Jiun Ho, conceived the space, suspending lights from an iron framework and exposing the oak beams. Starting at $248, the tasting menu is astronomical but the food is a revelation. Chef Joshua Skenes uses fish, aged meats and foraged vegetables in his creations, often topping them with caviar or abalone. Menus aren't released in advance, but that's all part of the intended experience. Diners should allow three hours for their meal, and book at least 60 days ahead.
178 Townsend Street, T 828 7990,
www.saisonsf.com

URBAN LIFE

CAFÉS, RESTAURANTS, BARS AND NIGHTCLUBS

San Francisco's oceanside location and the verdant land outside the city grant chefs access to some of the finest raw ingredients in the country. There's a vast array of exemplary places to eat out, from food trucks serving up tacos to Michelin-starred restaurants creating French cuisine with a Californian influence, and all display a reverence for the state's excellent wine and craft beers. Lately, a more experimental, locavore trend has swept through the city, at restaurants like Alta CA (see p048) and The Square (1707 Powell Street, T 525 3579), which both exude contemporary flair. Organic and sustainable Asian cooking is taken to a new level at Ramen Shop (5812 College Avenue, T 510 788 6370) in Oakland, and in The Mission, Dennis Lee adopts slow food principles to produce fine Korean cuisine at Namu Gaji (499 Dolores Street, T 431 6268).

Appealing bars are plentiful. Our picks are off the beaten path but worth the effort: try idiosyncratic venues such as Smuggler's Cove (650 Gough Street, T 869 1900) and Smokestack (2505 3rd Street, T 864 7468), where respected brewmaster Dave McLean makes the beer. The best clubs are not immediately obvious either, or as open as in London or New York, but there are lots of eclectic and interesting venues to be found; try Bergerac (316 11th Street, T 255 9440), a hip cocktail lounge where you can keep the party going upstairs at Audio Discotech (T 481 0556).

For full addresses, see Resources.

The Abbot's Cellar

The block between 18th and 19th Street has become an artisan hotbed, thanks to the presence of Dandelion Chocolate (T 349 0942), Mission Cheese (see p046) and The Abbot's Cellar. Decked out with rough-hewn wooden planks on the walls and tables designed by Tyler S Bradford, this is no average alehouse. There are about 20 beers on tap and 120 more in the cellar, each served with details about their provenance, the pour type (draft, bottle or cask) and tasting notes. The beers range from pale-golden lagers to barrel-aged stouts, as well as smoked, sour and gluten-free swigs. Co-owner and cellar master Christian Albertson collaborates with chef Adam Duyle on the four-course tasting menu.
742 Valencia Street, T 626 8700, www.abbotscellar.com

Atelier Crenn

French chef Dominique Crenn named this restaurant after her father's studio, and his artwork is displayed throughout the interior. Crenn has built a reputation for her modern take on French haute cuisine and her artistic, elegant presentation; to appreciate what she refers to as 'poetic culinaria', order one of the tasting menus; there's a signature seven-course or a more elaborate 18-course option, both of which can be teamed with wines (at an additional cost). The two-Michelin-starred Atelier Crenn was once credited as the best place in town to eat foie gras, before a city-wide ban on the product came into effect in 2012, but its ultra-seasonal fare still draws foodies. The wire chandeliers resembling birds' nests are a cool design element. *3127 Fillmore Street, T 440 0460, www.ateliercrenn.com*

Outerlands

Within its weathered fence and driftwood walls, this laidback restaurant near Ocean Beach, designed by owners David Muller and Lana Porcello, serves great organic cuisine: vegetable snacks like asparagus dip with crispy radishes and shallots, or charred cauliflower with cumin ricotta; hot and cold sandwiches, including classic grilled cheese or smoked confit chicken; and Dutch baby pancakes for weekend brunch. Drawn to its concise menu and fresh sourdough bread, which is baked in house and accompanies every meal, hungry surfers and beach-goers make up a fair proportion of the clientele. Despite an expansion in 2014 into the next-door space, formerly Wo's Chinese, the queues can still stretch round the block.
4001 Judah Street, T 661 6140,
www.outerlandssf.com

Mission Cheese
Among the unschooled, American cheese has had a bad rap in the past, but this is one of many fromageries in the city changing that tired perception. More than 60 varieties from diverse producers are available here. The café menu is chalked up on the board; try a grilled sandwich or the mac and cheese. *736 Valencia Street, T 553 8667, www.missioncheese.net*

Alta CA

Times are changing for the once blighted Mid-Market, a stretch between 6th and 12th Street, where firms including Twitter and Square have set up shop, bringing with them affluent techies in search of good food. Enter Alta CA, a laidback venue launched by restaurateur Daniel Patterson, who also owns Coi (T 393 9000), Ume (T 510 444 7586) and Haven (T 510 663 4440). Chef Yoni Levy's menu majors on innovative comfort foods, such as beef tendon puffs, slow-cooked pork shoulder, and chickpea and oxtail fritters. The simplicity of the cuisine is mirrored by the no-fuss, urban-industrial decor, which is punctuated by a floor-to-ceiling Russel Wright-inspired shelving system that separates the front and back of house. *1420 Market Street, T 590 2585, www.altaca.co*

Rich Table

Although this restaurant's name may lead you to think it pays homage to the Bay Area's celebrated fresh produce, it's actually named after husband-and-wife team Evan and Sarah Rich, who met while cooking at New York's Bouley. Having familiarised themselves with Californian cuisine, he at Coi (see p048) and she at Michael Mina (T 397 9222), they opened this 50-seat dinner-only establishment in 2012 as a temple to ingredient-driven dishes. Sardine chips, porcini doughnuts and rare pastas are specialities. Said-Jon Eghbal's interiors are in line with the locavore ethos: wood was sourced from a Petaluma sawmill, Jered's Pottery from Berkeley, and midcentury-inspired Heath Ceramics from Sausalito.
199 Gough Street, T 355 9085, www.richtablesf.com

Bouli Bar

The gourmet hub that is the Ferry Building has long been anchored by Boulettes Larder, an intimate restaurant known for its finely crafted food and interior. In 2013, design firm Kallos Turin applied the same ethos to Bouli Bar. Oversized Tom Dixon pendant lights, a brass bead curtain and American oak panelling set the right tone for Amaryll Schwertner's Eastern-influenced menu. Admire the airy 50-seat dining room while savouring the chef's delicate layering of textures and flavours; we highly recommend the Mediterranean salad with purslane, aged feta and pomegranate reduction. The menu features mezze options, and you can buy ingredients from Boulettes Larder next door to recreate the dishes at home.
1 Ferry Building, T 399 1177,
www.bouletteslarder.com

Tosca

In its heyday, Chinatown's Tosca was a dive bar, where politicians hung out with Beat poets and Hollywood starlets. In 2013, the place was relaunched as an Italian small-plates restaurant by Brit April Bloomfield, of The Spotted Pig and Breslin fame in New York. While much of the original decor remains the same, including the opera-playing jukebox, red booths and vintage espresso machine, the late-night revellers of old have been replaced by diehard foodies lining up for Bloomfield's bold cuisine. Isaac Shumway (formerly of Bourbon & Branch) heads up the bar, serving Tosca's house 'cappuccino', a Prohibition throwback made with milk, chocolate from Dandelion (see p041) and brandy, among other great cocktails. *242 Columbus Avenue, T 986 9651, www.toscacafesf.com*

The Slanted Door

One of the most acclaimed restaurants in a city renowned for its food, The Slanted Door played a major role in America's Asian fusion revolution. Reportedly, the buzz around the restaurant started when Bill and Chelsea Clinton arrived for lunch one day, at what was then a small and relatively unknown Vietnamese eaterie in The Mission. Today, it occupies a larger, more refined spot on The Embarcadero, overlooking the water. The menu has stayed pretty much the same, though, over the years; executive chef and owner Charles Phan draws on his Chinese roots, a childhood spent in Vietnam and, of course, California's ingredients. Try the wood-oven manila clams with thai basil, crispy pork belly and fresh chilli.
1 Ferry Building No 3, T 861 8032, www.slanteddoor.com

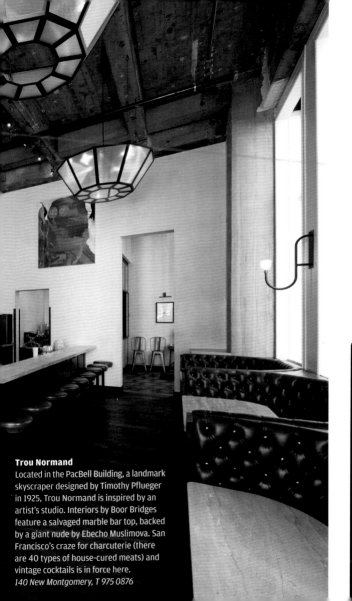

Trou Normand
Located in the PacBell Building, a landmark
skyscraper designed by Timothy Pflueger
in 1925, Trou Normand is inspired by an
artist's studio. Interiors by Boor Bridges
feature a salvaged marble bar top, backed
by a giant nude by Ebecho Muslimova. San
Francisco's craze for charcuterie (there
are 40 types of house-cured meats) and
vintage cocktails is in force here.
140 New Montgomery, T 975 0876

Quince

The Bay is brimming with restaurants run by highly skilled chefs who trained under slow-food pioneer Alice Waters at Chez Panisse (T 510 548 5525), but Michael Tusk is the current king of the pack, and Quince is the jewel in his crown. In 2009, the restaurant relocated from an intimate, 16-table venue in Pacific Heights to a larger, historic building downtown. But although the vibe has changed (the old place was a tad rarefied; the new space is much busier), everything that made Quince great is still present: unparalleled service and superb Italian- and French-influenced Northern Californian cuisine. Cotogna (T 775 8508), which Tusk launched next door to Quince, serves Italian cuisine and has a more casual ambience. *470 Pacific Avenue, T 775 8500, www.quincerestaurant.com*

Nopa

A giant folk-art mural by San Francisco-based painter Brian Barneclo, depicting scenes of Californian life, runs the length of Nopa's main wall. Complementing the restaurant's bohemian vibe, the menu places an emphasis on sustainable and organic produce, in dishes such as fresh pappardelle with spicy fennel sausage, peas, mint and pecorino. For drinks, there's a 10-page wine and sherry list to work your way through. Due to Nopa's popularity with locals, it's difficult to get a last-minute reservation here, but if you don't mind waiting it out around the large communal table, you'll likely get a spot eventually. If you can't, Nopa's sister restaurant, Nopalito (T 233 9966), serves Mexican food only a block away. *560 Divisadero Street, T 864 8643, www.nopasf.com*

Comal
City dwellers find themselves crossing
the bridge more often these days, and
Comal is a good reason to do so. At the
Cali-Oaxacan restaurant, Matt Gandin
makes some of the best mole north of
the border. Abueg Morris Architects
kept the original fir floor and installed
a 232 sq m patio; the art is by Deborah
O'Grady and John Bisbee (above).
2020 Shattuck Avenue, T 510 926 6300

Twenty Five Lusk

It can be hard to secure a dinner table at this celebrity haunt, but the lounge (left) is where you'll want to see and be seen anyway; arrive before 7pm to beat the crowds. Designed by San Francisco firm CCS Architecture, the space retains a strong sense of the building's history; it was originally a 1917 meatpacking house. The exposed brickwork, wooden beams and glass walls lend a contemporary industrial edge, enhanced by suspended fire pits and curved banquettes. The cocktails here are first-class and get rave reviews, especially the Manhattan. If you do get a reservation in the dining room, expect New American cuisine with a European slant, courtesy of Matthew Dolan, who trained with Emeril Lagasse.
25 Lusk Street, T 495 5875,
www.twentyfivelusk.com

INSIDER'S GUIDE

ECHE MARTINEZ, INTERIOR DESIGNER

Born in Buenos Aires, the cosmopolitan Eche Martinez arrived in San Francisco by way of Paris and Miami. Often a talking point in local creative circles, his interior design fuses bright colours and pop whimsy with a neoclassical elegance. On a typical morning, the Pacific Heights resident will jog to the base of the Golden Gate Bridge (see p012) to take in the spectacular views. Post-workout, he rewards himself with a vegan pastry from Greens (Fort Mason Building A, 2 Marina Boulevard, T 771 6222). At the weekend, his chosen brunch hangout is Nopa (see p057), where the French toast is 'worth every ounce of gluten and sugary deliciousness'.

One of his favourite walks is along Divisadero Street, location of antiques shop The Perish Trust (No 728), which hosts Umami Mart, 'a cute Japanese pop-up'. He also recommends Sacramento Street, for stores such as The Future Perfect (No 3085, T 932 6508) and March (see p084). 'To scout the perfect vintage chair', he heads to Past Perfect (2246 Lombard Street, T 929 2288).

Martinez's dinner hot-list includes Off the Grid's roving food trucks (www.offthegridsf.com) and Suzu Noodle House (1825 Post Street, T 346 5083), for 'Japanese comfort food at its finest'. After hours, he unwinds with a few cocktails at 1300 on Fillmore (1300 Fillmore Street, T 771 7100), or 'amazing locally brewed beers' at Magnolia Gastropub & Brewery (1398 Haight Street, T 864 7468). *For full addresses, see Resources.*

ARCHITOUR

A GUIDE TO SAN FRANCISCO'S ICONIC BUILDINGS

The city's first architectural golden age ended in rubble and smoke, when a powerful 1906 earthquake and subsequent fire destroyed much of San Francisco's Victorian infrastructure. Those buildings that did survive (you can see examples around Alamo Square and Liberty Hill) continued to define the built environment for years.

Change was signalled with SOM's 1964 One Maritime Plaza (300 Clay Street) and, in the early 1970s, Transamerica Pyramid (see p013). In the 21st century, Herzog & de Meuron's de Young Museum (see p070) created a halo effect, luring world-renowned architects like Rem Koolhaas and Norman Foster, who are both contributing to the Transbay Transit District, due to complete in 2017. Pelli Clarke Pelli is designing the transport centre itself, as well as the 326m Transbay Tower (415 Mission Street). Meanwhile, Gehry's Menlo Park Facebook headquarters is slated for 2015, and Foster's $5bn Apple complex in Cupertino for 2016.

The construction flurry has encompassed key cultural venues. Snøhetta's enlargement of SFMOMA (see p032) will be finished in 2016, while Mark Cavagnero's SFJazz Center (201 Franklin Street), and the restored ACT Strand Theater (1125 Market Street) are also of note. Projects in the pipeline include Michael Maltzan's Mashouf Performing Arts Center at SFSU's Lake Merced campus, and Diller Scofidio + Renfro's arts centres for Stanford and Berkeley. *For full addresses, see Resources.*

St Mary's Cathedral
One of the Catholic Church's boldest
20th-century statements, St Mary's was
conceived by Italian-American modernist
Pietro Belluschi, in collaboration with local
architects Angus McSweeney, Paul A Ryan
and John Michael Lee. Consecrated in 1971,
it has a travertine and concrete parabolic
exterior, which rises from a square base
to create a cross. The jaw-dropping interior
emphasises the form with stained-glass
windows that ascend on four sides and
converge at the apex. Sculptor Richard
Lippold designed the 45m-high baldachin
using more than 4,000 aluminium rods.
Soaring 57m from four concrete buttresses,
the structure was engineered by Pier Luigi
Nervi. The overall impression is one of
both drama and serenity.
1111 Gough Street, T 567 2020 ext 207,
www.stmarycathedralsf.org

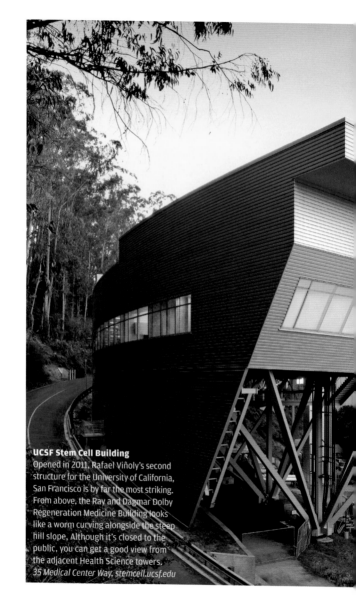

UCSF Stem Cell Building
Opened in 2011, Rafael Viñoly's second structure for the University of California, San Francisco is by far the most striking. From above, the Ray and Dagmar Dolby Regeneration Medicine Building looks like a worm curving alongside the steep hill slope. Although it's closed to the public, you can get a good view from the adjacent Health Science towers.
35 Medical Center Way. stemcell.ucsf.edu

California Academy of Sciences

As if it wasn't enough to have a Herzog & de Meuron-designed museum (see p070) in the middle of Golden Gate Park, Renzo Piano's California Academy of Sciences is just steps away, across the plaza. Best known for its undulating green roof and fabulous planetarium, the academy is some of the most environmentally friendly architecture in the country. Achieving high functionality was paramount in the water- and energy-efficient structure, given its inhabitants: a fascinating collection of butterflies, birds, reptiles, penguins and fish, all of which require tightly controlled temperature and light conditions to thrive. Spread out across the building's three floors are a shop, a 3D screen, restaurants and a lecture hall. *55 Music Concourse Drive, T 379 8000, www.calacademy.org*

Contemporary Jewish Museum

Daniel Libeskind's Contemporary Jewish Museum, opened in 2008, incorporates a former power station that had to remain in place due to planning laws. Libeskind's design drew inspiration from the Hebrew toast *L'chaim*, which means 'To life', and the concept is borne out on a number of levels. This was the city's main power plant (energy = life); the new element traces the shape of the Hebrew letters that form the word *chai* ('life'); and the museum itself celebrates the art and the history of the Jewish people. The dominant feature, two dark-blue steel planes, one on either side of the building, characterise the structure and block that it overshadows. Entry fees are waived on the first Tuesday of every month. Closed Wednesdays.
736 Mission Street, T 655 7800,
www.thecjm.org

de Young Museum

One of Herzog & de Meuron's most thought-provoking designs, the de Young is covered in perforated and textured copper, which creates the effect of light filtering through trees. As the facade ages and acquires a patina, it blends further into its surroundings. Tiers of windows, and unexpected angles and apertures inside the edifice blur the boundary between the interior and exterior, although the galleries themselves are more conventional in design, allowing the art to remain the most important presence. On the north-east side, the 44m-high tower has a glass-walled observation deck that affords great views over the park and the western side of San Francisco. *50 Hagiwara Tea Garden Drive, T 750 3600, deyoung.famsf.org*

SHOPPING

THE BEST RETAIL THERAPY AND WHAT TO BUY

San Francisco's shoppers are increasingly turning to handcrafted goods, a trend captured at furniture store The Future Perfect (see p062), kitchenware emporium March (see p084) and Oakland's Esqueleto gallery (482 49th Street, T 629 6216). Other specialist boutiques to seek out are No 3 (see p076), which sells jewellery, Jay Jeffers' interiors outlet Cavalier (1035 Post Street, T 440 7300), and Press Works on Paper (3108 24th Street, T 913 7156), which stocks new, used and first-edition books. Luxury fashion brands, like Marc Jacobs (No 125, T 362 6500) and Theory (No 120, T 399 1099), line the pedestrianised Maiden Lane; on chic Fillmore Street, Rag & Bone (No 2066) opened its first San Francisco store in 2014.

In this food utopia, edibles make great souvenirs. Buy gourmet treats at the Ferry Building (see p050); artisan chocolate from Fog City News (455 Market Street, T 543 7400); biodynamic wines at Terroir (1116 Folsom Street, T 558 9946); and for sustenance while you shop, sandwiches from Molinari Delicatessen (373 Columbus Avenue, T 421 2337). Rainbow Grocery Cooperative (1745 Folsom Street, T 863 0620) is the most right-on food store you'll ever visit.

Located in a former bowling alley, Amoeba Music (1855 Haight Street, T 831 1200), a sprawling indie shop, is a treasure trove of recorded product, while Aquarius Records (1055 Valencia Street, T 647 2272) is smaller but equally renowned.

For full addresses, see Resources.

CROOKED ST.
NORTH BEACH
FISHERMAN'S WHARF
USE LEFT LANE

The NWBLK

Located within a 1951 former factory space, The NWBLK (New Black) is an appointment-only gallery focusing on furniture, lighting and one-of-a-kind fashion pieces. Creative director and founder Steven Miller is as enthusiastic about local craftsmanship as the next retailer (see Chris Fraser's prints and Yaffe Mays' chair, overleaf), yet many pieces are by international designers, such as lighting from Melbourne's Christopher Boots, and furnishings by Swiss firm Strala and British/American designer Christopher Roy. Thanks to its industrial aesthetic, the cavernous interior lends itself to fashion events and parties, hosted by underground and established brands. At lunchtime, the outdoor yard becomes a gathering point for some of the city's finest food trucks.
1999 Bryant Street, T 621 2344, www.thenwblk.com

The NWBLK

No 3

Jenny Chung's retail outlets have injected some welcome sartorial sass into her native city. Whereas Chung's other store, Acrimony (T 861 1025), is dedicated to mens- and womenswear, No 3 is wholly focused on jewellery, displaying each designer's collection in a glass terrarium created by local craftsman Conor Sweitzer. Expect an assemblage of sculptural pieces, such as the edgy chevron cuffs and collars by LA's Tomtom, and more delicate items, like filigree rings adorned with diamonds from Vale, and an interlocking puzzle ring by New York brand Bliss Lau. If you are thinking of popping the question, Chung will be more than happy to assist with an assortment of unorthodox engagement rings and singular settings.
1987 Hyde Street/Union Street, T 525 4683, www.shopno3.com

Self Edge

Specialising in Japanese selvedge denim (Iron Heart, The Flat Head, 3sixteen), Self Edge is a fun space to visit even if you're not in the market for dropping several hundred dollars on a pair of jeans. It stocks an impressive variety of brands that are rarely seen outside Japan, although there are more options for men than women. Complimentary hemming is available on all purchases, achieved with a vintage chain-stitching machine. The denim range is the focal point, but there's also a good selection of men's shirts and accessories. Founded in 2006 by Bay Area husband-and-wife team Kiya and Demitra Babzani, Self Edge has proved a real hit, and has expanded across the States, with outlets in New York, Los Angeles and Portland. *714 Valencia Street, T 558 0658, www.selfedge.com*

Local Mission Market
Sourcing produce solely from Northern
California, Local Mission Market has oak
bins filled with grains, chillies and fruit;
its butcher's counter is an education
in sustainable farming; and its aisles are
lined with everything from bread, pasta
and crackers to condiments and fish.
The list of suppliers reads like a who's
who of the area's organic farmers.
2670 Harrison Street, T 795 3355

49 Geary Street

The five storeys of 49 Geary Street, not far from Union Square, are home to several of San Francisco's most notable art galleries. Each one has its own focus, although the majority show modern photography. Not so the Bekris Gallery (above; T 513 5154), on the second floor, which stands out for its emphasis on a broad range of disciplines (sculpture, illustration and multimedia installations) and work from Africa. Make time to visit the Fraenkel Gallery (see p036), whose exhibitions have spotlighted seminal American photographers, such as Irving Penn, Lee Friedlander and Nan Goldin; and the third-floor Stephen Wirtz Gallery (T 433 6879), which presents a varied selection of visual art. Many of the 19 independent venues here stay open late on the first Thursday of the month.

William Stout Architectural Books

There's no telling how this bookshop, dedicated to architecture, art and design, stays open in the age of Amazon, but it doesn't seem to be going anywhere any time soon. Just a block away from the Transamerica Pyramid (see p013), it was founded by architect William Stout more than three decades ago. On his return from Europe, books unavailable in San Francisco in hand, he found that friends would ask him to acquire copies for them too. Today, the store is stuffed with tomes that run the gamut of creative subjects, from graphic design and typography to landscaping and the decorative arts. The knowledgeable staff are always happy to answer questions, help you find a rare publication or simply leave you to browse. *804 Montgomery Street, T 391 6757, www.stoutbooks.com*

General Store

Within earshot of the Pacific's crashing
waves, this multifaceted boutique, located
in the Outer Sunset neighbourhood, stocks
everything a crystal-gazing, West Coast
soul surfer could possibly desire, from
vintage, Navajo-patterned Pendleton
blankets and hand-knitted wool caps, to
homewares such as Luke Bartels' locally
made rustic chopping boards. Kathleen
Whitaker's jewellery, Postalco stationery
and Morgan Parish leather goods line
the walls and the store's quirky wooden
tunnel, built by architect Mason St Peter,
who runs the shop with his wife, Serena
Mitnik-Miller. If you're looking for a gift for
a Californian friend, consider one of the
plants for sale in the greenhouse, which
was designed by artist Jesse Schlesinger
and is tucked away in the backyard.
4035 Judah Street, T 682 0600,
www.shop-generalstore.com

March

Pots and pans assume art/design-object status at March, where Sam Hamilton sells skilfully crafted kitchenware made from the finest materials. Top-quality goods, such as Brickett Davda's handmade bowls, Blackcreek Mercantile & Trading's wooden spoons and March's own-brand kosher salt (above), $80, are beautiful products that epitomise the clean-lined Californian aesthetic. The showroom is laid out like a kitchen, with gleaming stainless-steel and copper fixtures, bespoke butcher-block tables from Union Studio's Matt Bear and a cherrywood bench by Sawkille (opposite), made to order from $5,600. Hanging on the walls are the marbled-ribeye paintings of Carrie Mae Smith alongside photos by New York-based Paulette Tavormina. *3075 Sacramento Street, T 931 7433, www.marchsf.com*

Xanadu Gallery
Established in 1979, this eclectic gallery,
just off Union Square in San Francisco's
only Frank Lloyd Wright building, stocks
antiques and art sourced from across
the world. On display in Wright's proto-
Guggenheim are covetable artefacts,
textiles, artwork and jewellery from
Oceania, Africa, Asia and Latin America.
*140 Maiden Lane, T 392 9999,
www.xanadugallery.us*

SPORTS AND SPAS
WORK OUT, CHILL OUT OR JUST WATCH

The citizens of San Francisco are serious about sport and fitness, and thanks to the city's topography, the daily commute can be akin to an intense StairMaster workout. You'll easily spot them, as they stroll casually past red-faced visitors huffing and puffing their way up the punishing inclines of the steeper streets. The fittest local cycle couriers would surely measure up against many professional riders. And unless you're Chris Froome-fit, save the rental bike for crossing the Golden Gate Bridge (see p012).

San Francisco is blessed with an abundance of beaches in and around town, and surfing is a serious and all-consuming pursuit. The Pacific can be notoriously dangerous at the city's Ocean Beach, which has frigid surf and powerful tides. The waves are gentler a short drive away at Linda Mar Beach (see p090) and, a little further south, in laidback Santa Cruz. Over in Half Moon Bay, the legendary Mavericks wave break draws the world's best-known and most skilled surfers for an annual competition.

Surprisingly for a US city this size, San Francisco lacks an NBA team (cross the bridge to Oakland for that), making baseball and football the major sports here. Your hotel concierge should be able to procure tickets to a Giants (see p094) or a 49ers game – down Route 101 at Levi's Stadium (4900 Marie P Bartolo Way, Santa Clara, T 464 9377) – which are great spectacles, even for the uninitiated. *For full addresses, see Resources.*

JA's Razor Club

Opened in 2013, this discreet salon for men is situated on the mezzanine level of John Varvatos' boutique in Union Square. The industrial beams, red-brick walls and black-leather chairs announce there is nothing remotely camp about this 213 sq m clubhouse. Most of the patrons have memberships, although anyone can make an appointment for a treatment, such as the signature 'Legend', which comprises a massaging shampoo, conditioning treatment, cut, cooling rinse, hot-towel steam and facial cleanse, all packed into 45 minutes. Services are rounded off with a shoe-shine, and there's a selection of complimentary beverages to quaff, ensuring customers leave with a skip in their immaculately groomed step. *152 Geary Street, T 398 2707, www.johnallans.com*

Linda Mar Beach, Pacifica

Surfing in Northern California is different from the Southern Californian variety in many respects, but the major contrast is the climate. Twenty minutes outside San Francisco, Linda Mar, aka Pacifica State, is a good option for novices and more experienced boarders. Beginners typically arrive in the morning; Adventure Out (T 1 800 509 3954) runs one-, two- and four-day courses. Wearing a wetsuit is essential; Adventure Out will provide one if you book a lesson, or there are surf shops near the beach where you can rent one, and a board for that matter. The waves are mellow but the weather isn't: fog and wind are as inescapable as the tide. Even if you don't surf, Linda Mar is a beautiful place to go to relax and watch everyone else hang ten.

Cabrillo Highway/Linda Mar Boulevard

Mission Cliffs

If the near-vertical hills in some parts of the city aren't enough of a challenge for you, this venue will be, whether you're a first-timer or a diehard rock jock. Mission Cliffs is operated by Touchstone Climbing, which now runs nine such indoor facilities across California. This is the original and the most impressive of its rock-climbing centres, and has a main wall more than 15m high, with 140 roped routes and lots more on the lower, boulder terrain. A 465 sq m expansion in 2014 underlined the scale of the place. There's an upward path to suit everyone, but if you do lose your head for heights, the yoga studio, cardiovascular room and indoor cycling programme also guarantee a workout. Day passes can be purchased for $20. *2295 Harrison Street, T 550 0515, www.touchstoneclimbing.com*

International Orange

In Pacific Heights, above the shopping bustle of Fillmore, International Orange offers a tranquil escape from the crowds. Within the crisp white interior, which features natural stone and reclaimed-wood floors, many of the city's leading massage therapists and beauticians administer soothing treatments, including 90-minute hot-stone or Thai massages, aromatic scalp therapies and reflexology. Acupuncture sessions are also available. The retail area stocks a good range of cult beauty products by brands such as May Lindstrom and SkinCeuticals, as well as the Hollywood favourite Arcona. The venue has a strong reputation for its yoga classes, which are held daily in the spacious, airy studio (above).
Second floor, 2044 Fillmore Street, T 563 5000, www.internationalorange.com

AT&T Park

This is a city with a proud sporting history; those who have pulled on the jersey for the San Francisco Giants include baseball legends Willie Mays and Barry Bonds. If you can score tickets to a home game (even harder to come by since the team's 2012 World Series win), take a trip to AT&T Park in South Beach and soak up the atmosphere. Perched on the waterfront at the southern end of The Embarcadero, the views beyond the diamond and out to San Francisco Bay make this one of the most dramatic settings for Major League Baseball. If a slugger takes the plate and really connects, you might be lucky enough to see the ball go flying over the wall and into the McCovey Cove beyond, where enterprising kayakers gather with waterproof radios to listen to the game and paddle for 'splash hits'.

24 Willie Mays Plaza, T 972 2000, www.sfgiants.com

ESCAPES

WHERE TO GO IF YOU WANT TO LEAVE TOWN

The landscape surrounding San Francisco is some of the most arresting in America. Admire it by renting a bike and cycling north over the Golden Gate Bridge (see p012), to the vantage point on the far side overlooking the city, or beyond to the Marin Headlands and Rodeo Beach, where you can visit Headlands Center for the Arts (944 Simmonds Road, Sausalito, T 331 2787). For shady respite and a sublime connection with nature, make for Muir Woods in Mill Valley, 19km north of the bridge. The area's majestic redwoods are some of the tallest and oldest trees on the planet.

One of the world's greatest drives is south from the city down the Pacific Coast Highway to Carmel and Big Sur. Stop for a walk along the beautiful Pfeiffer Beach, refuelling at Big Sur Bakery & Restaurant (47540 Highway 1, T 831 667 0520). Perched in a stunning location, 365m above the Pacific, Post Ranch Inn (47900 Highway 1, T 888 524 4787) is on the bucket list of most SF residents.

North of town is wine country. Choosing between Sonoma (see p102) and Napa is hard; you may opt for the latter because of its storied history. Travel along the Silverado Trail, stopping at Pine Ridge (No 5901, T 707 252 9777) to taste its highly regarded cabernet sauvignon. In nearby Yountville, Thomas Keller's three-Michelin-starred restaurant French Laundry (6640 Washington Street, T 707 944 2380; reservations essential) is a culinary legend.
For full addresses, see Resources.

Point Reyes National Seashore

Many beaches and nature reserves lie just outside the city, but Point Reyes National Seashore is one of the most spectacular. Some 50km north of San Francisco, open grassland and forested cliffs tower above vast stretches of sand. Some beaches here, such as Stinson, are family-oriented and are good for swimming, while others, like McClures, where the surf is treacherous, are more thrilling. Wildlife is abundant in the area; look out for pelicans, eagles and elk. Coastal walks and kayaking trips can be arranged at Point Reyes Outdoors (T 663 8192). Grey whales' migratory path takes these magnificent mammals up this coast, and at the right time of year, usually February, you can spot them from the historic Point Reyes Lighthouse (above) at the tip of the peninsula.
www.nps.gov/pore

Marin County Civic Center

Frank Lloyd Wright's last design, the Marin County Civic Center is 32km north of San Francisco. Completed after the architect's death by his protégé Aaron Green, and situated on an old dairy farm, the building bears all of Wright's hallmarks. The arches, dome and cut-outs echo the topography of the site, and the sandy colour of the walls resembles the shade of the earth. Inside, corridors with rounded corners create the illusion of a continuous circular space. The most distinctive feature, a 52.4m gold-anodised spire, separates the hall of justice and administration wings. Time your visit to coincide with Marin's oldest farmers' market, held on Thursday and Sunday mornings in the car park, but due to receive a permanent $20m plot. *10 Avenue of the Flags, T 473 6400, www.marincounty.org*

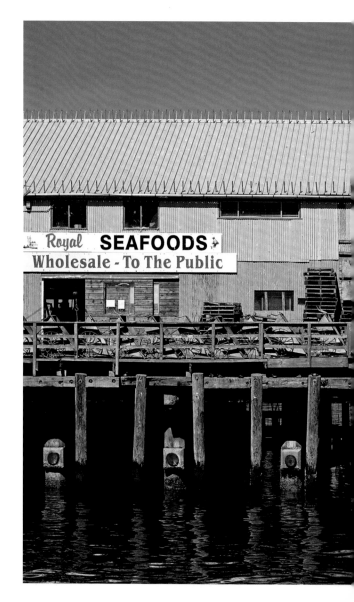

Cannery Row, Monterey
Once the centre of the sardine canning
industry, as immortalised in the novel
by former resident John Steinbeck, the
alluring oceanside town of Monterey is
two hours' drive south of San Francisco.
Its labyrinth of ramshackle warehouses,
jutting out over the ocean, has now been
colonised by pleasingly nostalgic bars,
restaurants and, arguably, the nation's
finest aquarium (T 831 648 4800).

Ram's Gate, Sonoma

Located off Highway 121 at the gateway to Sonoma, this winery is architect Howard Backen's contemporary interpretation of a traditional farmstead. The interiors are the work of Orlando Diaz-Azcuy, who used a combination of vintage and bespoke furnishing to create a relaxed but modish setting for tasting and events. Continue on your tour to the nearby biodynamic Scribe Winery (T 707 939 1858), known for its hipsters as much as its chardonnay. For a bite, El Dorado Kitchen (T 800 289 3031) and The Girl & The Fig (T 707 938 3634) are solid bets. Further north, Healdsburg lures the design-savvy to the gallery Lulo (T 707 433 7533), Cartograph tasting room (T 707 433 8270) and Jensen Architects-designed café/store Shed (T 707 431 7433). *28700 Arnold Drive, T 707 721 8700, www.ramsgatewinery.com*

NOTES
SKETCHES AND MEMOS

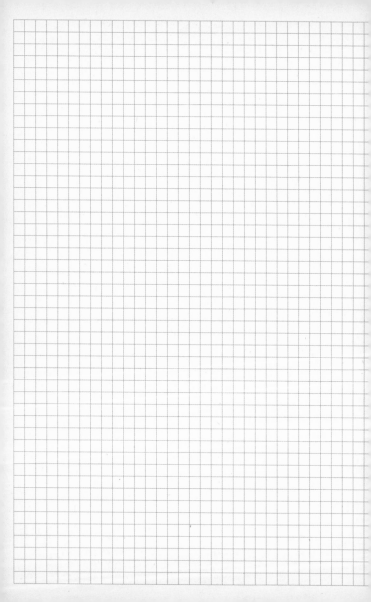

RESOURCES
CITY GUIDE DIRECTORY

A

The Abbot's Cellar 041
742 Valencia Street
T 626 8700
www.abbotscellar.com

Acrimony 076
333 Hayes Street
T 861 1025
www.shopacrimony.com

ACT Strand Theatre 064
1125 Market Street
T 415 749 2228
www.act-sf.org

Adventure Out 090
T 1 800 509 3954
www.adventureout.com

Alcatraz Cruises 035
Pier 33
Alcatraz Landing
T 981 7625
www.alcatrazcruises.com

Alta CA 048
1420 Market Street
T 590 2585
www.altaca.co

Ame 025
St Regis
125 3rd Street
T 284 4040
www.amerestaurant.com

Americano 027
Hotel Vitale
8 Mission Street
T 278 3777
www.hotelvitale.com

Amoeba Music 072
1855 Haight Street
T 831 1200
www.amoeba.com

Aquarius Records 072
1055 Valencia Street
T 647 2272
www.aquariusrecords.org

AT&T Park 094
4 Willie Mays Plaza
T 972 2000
www.sfgiants.com

Atelier Crenn 044
3127 Fillmore Street
T 440 0460
www.ateliercrenn.com

Audio Discotech 040
316 11th Street
T 481 0556
www.audiosf.com

B

Bekris Gallery 080
49 Geary Street
T 513 5154
www.bekrisgallery.com

Bergerac 040
316 11th Street
T 255 9440
www.bergeracsf.com

Big Sur Bakery & Restaurant 096
47540 Highway 1
Big Sur
T 831 667 0520
www.bigsurbakery.com

Bliss Spa 018
W
181 3rd Street
T 817 4101
www.blissworld.com

HOTELS

ADDRESSES AND ROOM RATES

Clift 024
Room rates:
double, from $550;
Room 309, $530;
Studio Room, $600
495 Geary Street
T 775 4700
www.clifthotel.com

The Fairmont 016
Room rates:
double, from $470
950 Mason Street
T 772 5000
www.fairmont.com/sanfrancisco

Hotel G 020
Room rates:
double, from $250;
Greatest King, from $250
386 Geary Street
T 738 0589
www.hotelgsanfrancisco.com

Inn at the Presidio 016
Room rates:
double from $220
42 Moraga Avenue
T 800 7356
www.innatthepresidio.com

InterContinental 030
Room rates:
double, from $250;
One-Bedroom Corner
Suite 3006, from $1,200
888 Howard Street
T 616 6500
www.intercontinentalsanfrancisco.com

Mandarin Oriental 016
Room rates:
double, from $885
222 Sansome Street
T 276 9888
www.mandarinoriental.com/sanfrancisco

Mystic Hotel 023
Room rates:
double, from $260;
Mystic Junior Suite, $370
417 Stockton Street
T 400 0500
www.mystichotel.com

Orchard Garden Hotel 016
Room rates:
double, from $300
466 Bush Street
T 399 9807
www.theorchardgardenhotel.com

Palace Hotel 029
Room rates:
double, from $630;
Chancellor Suite, $1,030
2 New Montgomery Street
T 512 1111
www.sfpalace.com

Post Ranch Inn 096
Room rates:
Butterfly Room, from $675
47900 Highway 1
Big Sur
T 888 524 4787
www.postranchinn.com

St Regis 025
Room rates:
double, from $830;
Superior Room, $830
125 3rd Street
T 284 4000
www.stregissanfrancisco.com

Taj Campton Place 028
Room rates:
double, from $730;
Luxury Suite 1702, $2,700
340 Stockton Street
T 781 5555
www.tajhotels.com

Hotel Tomo 016
Room rates:
double, from $145
1800 Sutter Street
T 921 4000
www.jdvhotels.com

Hotel Vertigo 022
Room rates:
double, $150;
Executive King, from $170
940 Sutter Street
T 885 6800
www.hotelvertigosf.com

Hotel Vitale 026
Room rates:
double, from $930;
Deluxe City View Room, $810;
Cielo Terrace Suite, $1,000
8 Mission Street
T 278 3700
www.hotelvitale.com

W 018
Room rates:
double, from $730;
Cool Corner Room, $800;
Fantastic Suite, $2,500
181 3rd Street
T 777 5300
www.wsanfrancisco.com

Hotel Zetta 017
Room rates:
double, from $380;
Premier Studio King, from $440;
suite, from $900
55 5th Street
T 543 8555
www.hotelzetta.com

WALLPAPER* CITY GUIDES

Executive Editor
Rachael Moloney

Editor
Ella Marshall

Author
Cheryl Locke

Art Editor
Eriko Shimazaki
Original Design
Loran Stosskopf
Map Illustrator
Russell Bell

Photography Editor
Elisa Merlo
**Assistant Photography
Editor**
Nabil Butt

Production Manager
Vanessa Todd-Holmes

Chief Sub-Editor
Nick Mee
Sub-Editor
Farah Shafiq

Editorial Assistant
Emilee Jane Tombs

Contributors
William Bostwick
Charlie Lu
Amy Westervelt

Interns
Marina Hartung
Rosemary Stopher

Wallpaper* ® is a
registered trademark
of IPC Media Limited

First published 2007
Revised and updated
2010, 2011, 2012 and 2014

© Phaidon Press Limited

All prices are correct at
the time of going to press,
but are subject to change.

Printed in China

Phaidon Press Limited
Regent's Wharf
All Saints Street
London N1 9PA

Phaidon Press Inc
65 Bleecker Street
New York, NY 10012

Phaidon® is a registered
trademark of Phaidon
Press Limited

www.phaidon.com

A CIP Catalogue record for
this book is available from
the British Library.

ISBN 978 0 7148 6840 0

PHOTOGRAPHERS

SAN FRANCISCO

A COLOUR-CODED GUIDE TO THE HOT 'HOODS

NORTH BEACH
Theatregoers, diners and nightclubbers are all drawn to Little Italy's lively scene

NOB HILL
Head to one of America's most affluent areas for some of the finest panoramas in town

HAIGHT-ASHBURY
Although this hippy 'hood has lost its lustre, it's worth swinging by its infamous hub

SOMA
The city's leading cultural institutions cluster together in this centrally located district

CHINATOWN
Fast-paced and fascinating, this is the biggest and oldest Chinese enclave in the US

THE CASTRO
It's party central in California's exuberant gay heartland, so arrive with an open mind

THE MISSION
Modern art, fashionable bars and designer stores have taken over the Spanish quarter

HAYES VALLEY
Lined with unique boutiques, the central street here is a shopaholic's dream come true

For a full description of each neighbourhood, see the Introduction.
Featured venues are colour-coded, according to the district in which they are located.